THE CIVIL WAR

ON TO RICHMOND

The Civil War in the East, 1861-1862

James R. Arnold and Roberta Wiener

LERNER PUBLICATIONS COMPANY • MINNEAPOLIS

**First American edition published in 2002
by Lerner Publications Company**

Copyright © 2002 by Lerner Publications Company

The Civil War series is created and produced by Graham Beehag Books, in cooperation with Lerner Publications Company, a division of Lerner Publishing Group.

Lerner Publications Company
A division of Lerner Publishing Group
241 First Avenue North
Minneapolis, Minnesota 55401 U.S.A.

Website address: www.lernerbooks.com

Library of Congress Cataloging-in-Publication Data

Arnold, James R.
  On to Richmond : the Civil War in the East, 1861–1862 / by James R. Arnold and Roberta Wiener.
    p. cm. – (The Civil War)
Includes bibliographical references and index.
  ISBN 0-8225-2313-2 (lib. bdg. : alk. paper)
  1. Virginia—History—Civil War, 1861–1865—Campaigns—Juvenile literature. 2. United States—History—Civil War, 1861–1865—Campaigns—Juvenile literature. 3. Richmond (Va.)—History—Civil War, 1861-1865—Juvenile literature.
  4. Lincoln, Abraham, 1809–1865—Juvenile literature. 5. Lee, Robert E. (Robert Edward), 1807–1870—Juvenile literature.
  6. McClellan, George Brinton, 1826–1885—Juvenile literature.
  [1.Virginia—History—Civil War, 1861–1865—Campaigns. 2. United States—History—Civil War, 1861–1865—Campaigns.] I. Wiener, Roberta, 1952- II. Title. III. Civil War (Minneapolis, Minn.)
  E470.2 .A76   2002
  973.7'3—dc21   00-012184

Printed in Singapore
Bound in the United States of America
1 2 3 4 5 6 – OS – 07 06 05 04 03 02

The authors are grateful to Kate Kjorlien, whose excellent editing of the manuscript has made this book such a pleasure to read.

Front cover picture: *Battle of Antietam, near Sharpsburg, Maryland, 1862*

Back cover picture: *Dead soldiers after the Battle of Antietam*

Contents

WORDS YOU NEED TO KNOW

(For an explanation of *battery*, *brigade*, *company*, *corps*, *division*, and *regiment*, please refer to "A Civil War Army" on pages 64–65.)

army: a large group of soldiers organized to fight a war

artillery: a group of cannons and other large guns used by armies to fire at enemy soldiers

bayonet: a sword attached to the front of a musket or other gun

campaign: a series of military actions, such as marches and battles, to capture a certain place

cavalry: a group of soldiers who move and fight on horseback

civilian: a person who is not in the army or navy

desertion: leaving the army without permission

flank: one side of a group of soldiers

infantry: soldiers who move and fight on foot

militia: a group of people not normally part of the army who organize and arm themselves. Militias are formed in emergencies, for the purpose of defending their homeland.

morale: the confidence, courage, and fighting spirit of soldiers

musket: a type of gun used by foot soldiers before rifles became commonly used. Muskets are not as accurate as rifles in hitting a target.

navy: the part of the military that fights on the sea. It is made up of sailors and ships armed with cannons.

officer: a soldier of high rank who is in charge of other soldiers. To be called an officer, a soldier must at least have the rank of lieutenant. The higher officer ranks are captain, major, colonel, and general. The lower ranks, which are not officers, are private, corporal, and sergeant.

rank: the level of job held by a soldier, such as private, corporal, sergeant, colonel, or general

shell: a type of ammunition fired by artillery guns. It is a hollow case filled with explosives and pieces of metal.

strategy: the overall plan for organizing soldiers to fight a battle

surrender: to stop fighting and give in to the other side

theater: the geographical area in which a battle is fought

unit: an organized group of soldiers

INTRODUCTION
Two Nations Go to War

The Northern states and the Southern states had been growing apart for many years. They disagreed about whether slavery was right or wrong. They also disagreed about whether the Southern states had the right to leave the United States of America.

Then Abraham Lincoln won the election of 1860 and became the president of the United States. The Southern states disliked Lincoln. They feared that he would force them to give up owning slaves. As soon as Lincoln was elected, South Carolina seceded from, or left, the United States. Other Southern states quickly followed. Early in 1861, these states formed their own nation: the Confederate States of America, also called the Confederacy. Citizens of this new nation called themselves Confederates. They chose Jefferson Davis as their president. The Confederates believed that they had to fight the North to win their independence.

Northerners called the Southerners rebels, because the South had rebelled, or revolted, against the North. Northerners called their states the Union. They wanted to keep both Northern and Southern states unified, or together, as one nation. And Northerners were willing to fight to accomplish this goal. So the war began.

CHAPTER ONE

Collision at Bull Run

After Confederate soldiers captured Fort Sumter on April 14, 1861, the Civil War began. President Abraham Lincoln asked that 75,000 men enlist, or sign up, to fight against the Confederacy. These soldiers were supposed to fight for three months. Lincoln didn't think the war would last any longer. In the South, Confederate president Jefferson Davis made plans to form an army of 100,000 men to fight against the Union.

Men in the North joined the Union army. Southern men joined the Confederate army. But these young men were civilians, people

Alabama soldiers arriving in Richmond, above, *to join the Confederate army*

A Confederate soldier leaving for the war, right. *The child on the floor holds a Confederate flag. Sad scenes of soldiers saying good-bye were popular subjects for paintings at this time.*

who had never fought in a war. They traveled to camps, in the North and the South, to learn how to fight.

Both sides lacked experienced leaders. At the start of the Civil War, the U.S. Army had 1,080 officers (men who hold rank, or position, and lead other soldiers).

None of the officers had ever commanded large groups of men. But some officers had been in battles before. They had fought in the Mexican

A Union officer says good-bye to his family.

General Pierre Gustave Toutant Beauregard, right, *was from Louisiana. As a U.S. soldier, he had studied at the U.S. Military Academy at West Point, New York. After joining the Confederate army, Beauregard commanded the Confederate forces that bombarded Fort Sumter at the beginning of the war.*

War from 1846 to 1848. This experience helped. But their knowledge of war was old. Many things had changed since the 1840s.

Other officers had been in fights against Indian peoples in the American West. These fights had been skirmishes, or small battles, with only a few dozen men on each side. The problems of leading 20 men were very different from the problems of leading 2,000 or 20,000 men.

And some officers had never been in a battle. They became officers because they were good politicians or because they had powerful friends. This type of officer is called a political general. Very few political generals turned out to be good leaders.

Each officer faced a decision about whether to join the North or the South. Most born in the North joined the Union army. Most born in the South joined the Confederate army. Before the Civil War, these men had thought of themselves as brothers. Now they split apart and got ready to fight one another.

Soldiers on both sides were unprepared for battle. Most of the men were new, inexperienced soldiers. They were frightened. They worried about being hurt or killed. Their fellow soldiers were their friends and neighbors. If a soldier acted like a coward, these men would notice. They would tell the folks back home. Parents, other relatives, and friends would all hear the news. It would be hard to return home and live with the shame. A Texas soldier wrote to his mother before his first battle, "I may run but if I do I wish that some of our men would shoot me down." The fear of acting like a coward made men act bravely.

A group of Virginia Military Institute cadets (soldiers in training) photographed just before the Civil War began

The South had one important advantage over the North. It had military academies, or schools, such as the Virginia Military Institute (VMI) and the South Carolina Military Academy (The Citadel). At these academies, young men learned about military discipline, or how to behave on the battlefield. Their teachers taught them about military strategy, or how to plan to win a battle.

When the war began, men who had graduated from, or finished, these military schools joined the Southern armies. Younger boys who were still students also were useful. For example, on drill

Virginia soldiers, below. Waiting for the battle to begin was very hard. Men were excited and nervous. A soldier reported, "With your first shot you become a new man. Personal safety is your least concern."

fields outside of Richmond, Virginia, VMI teenagers taught older men how to march and how to use weapons.

Meanwhile, in the capital city of the Union—Washington, D.C.—Lincoln met with Northern political leaders. They met to create a strategy for how to fight against the South. They looked at their maps and saw that there would be two main theaters, or areas, where the war would be

fought: Virginia (the eastern theater) and the Mississippi-Tennessee River area (the western theater). Northern leaders decided to begin in the eastern theater, with an invasion of the South.

Lincoln and his generals thought that the South's capital—Richmond, Virginia—was the most important place to capture. But the generals wanted time to train their men before starting this invasion.

Volunteers marched to war often carrying far too much. A Massachusetts volunteer described what he carried in his knapsack: "a pair of trousers, two pairs of drawers [underwear], a pair of thick boots, four pairs of stockings, four flannel shirts, a blouse, a looking-glass [mirror], a can of peaches, a bottle of cough-mixture . . . razor and . . . a Bible, a small volume of Shakespeare, and writing utensils. To its top was strapped a double woolen blanket and a rubber one."

The people in the North wanted the war to end quickly. They wanted Lincoln to attack the South right away. The cry "On to Richmond!" grew so strong that Lincoln decided the army had to move.

Confederate president Jefferson Davis and Southern political leaders also planned for the war. They decided to keep their soldiers in the South. That way, if the Union army attacked, Confederate soldiers could defend Southern cities, their homes, and their families.

Each side had two groups of soldiers in Virginia. Major General Irvin McDowell commanded, or led, about 30,000 Union soldiers near Washington, D.C. General Robert Patterson commanded

Southern women offer soldiers refreshments as they board the train to travel to Manassas, Virginia. Places like Manassas Junction, where railroads joined, were important during the Civil War. Trains carried supplies to the Union and Confederate armies.

NAMING BATTLES

Many Civil War battles have two names. The North usually named a battle after a nearby stream or river. The South usually named it after a nearby town.

Northern Name	Southern Name
First Battle of Bull Run	First Manassas
Second Battle of Bull Run	Second Manassas
Battle of Antietam	Battle of Sharpsburg

Tennessee soldiers march to war. A young Southern volunteer wrote to his mother, "If the North [beats] the South I never want to live to be 21 years old."

another group of Union soldiers near Harpers Ferry, Virginia. General Joseph E. Johnston commanded Confederate soldiers also near Harpers Ferry. And General Pierre Beauregard commanded a second group of Confederate soldiers. They guarded the important railroad town of Manassas, about twenty-five miles southwest of Washington, D.C.

Patterson's Union army worked to keep Johnston's Confederate army from moving. Meanwhile, McDowell's Union army marched south toward Richmond. On its way, it collided

General Irvin McDowell commanded the Union army at the First Battle of Bull Run.

with Beauregard's Confederate army near a small creek known as Bull Run. There Northern and Southern soldiers fought the First Battle of Bull Run on July 21, 1861.

The First Battle of Bull Run

McDowell made a good plan. He sent part of his Union army straight toward Beauregard's Confederate army. The Union soldiers would divert, or distract, the Confederates. Meanwhile, the rest of McDowell's soldiers would outflank (march around and behind) a section of the Confederate army. McDowell hoped his move to outflank Beauregard would surprise and defeat the Confederates.

McDowell's soldiers learned that they were about to fight a battle. Thomas B. Barker, a soldier from Maine, wrote to his younger brother: "We are to move on to attack them tomorrow. . . . Many will be slain [killed] . . . and I am as likely to fall [be killed] as anyone. But . . . I am content to take whatever is to come. Should I be slain you will then be the eldest left and I doubt not you will fill my place." Thomas Barker died in battle the next day.

At 9:30 A.M. on July 21, the Union army began to march around the Confederates. A Confederate leader, Colonel Nathan Evans, moved a small group of soldiers to try to stop the Union army. The first fight of Bull Run happened on

Matthews Hill. A Confederate soldier described what he saw: "I looked towards the enemy and ...the balls [bullets] just poured on us, struck our muskets [guns] and hats and bodies."

Evans's men fought hard and slowed the Union army. But Evans needed help. Units, or groups, of soldiers marched to help Evans. General Barnard Bee commanded them. They had traveled by train to reach the battlefield. It was the first time in history that soldiers had used a train to move quickly to a battlefield. Bee's arrival was a surprise to the Union officers. They thought these men were still miles away in Virginia's Shenandoah Valley.

Bee's men helped Evans's men defend, or protect, Matthews Hill. But McDowell ordered more attacks. One of McDowell's officers, William T. Sherman, led Union soldiers across Bull Run. Sherman's men marched toward the Confederates on Matthews Hill. This forced the Confederates to fight in two directions at once.

UNDERSTANDING CASUALTIES

The word *casualties* refers to soldiers who are either killed, wounded, captured by the enemy, or missing as the result of a battle. When somebody is missing after a battle, a couple of things could have happened. The soldier could have been killed, but nobody could find or recognize the body. Or the soldier could have been captured and nobody knows where the soldier is.

Civil War casualties reached about 620,000. This is a very high number of American casualties when compared to wars of the twentieth century. In World War II, in which the United States fought from 1941 to 1945, 235,000 American soldiers were killed in battle. Another 701,000 were wounded, captured, or missing. During the Vietnam War, in which the United States fought from 1965 to 1973, about 58,000 Americans were killed.

17

It was more than they could do. Shortly before 12:00 P.M., Evans and Bee gave up Matthews Hill and moved to Henry House Hill. Union soldiers followed them. Whoever captured Henry House Hill would win the battle.

The Union army attacked again and again. By 2:00 P.M., the Confederates could barely hold on to Henry House Hill. Bee rode his horse over to a brigadier general named Thomas Jonathan Jackson. Bee said, "General, they are beating us back."

Jackson sternly replied, "Sir, we'll give them the bayonet [a knife attached to the end of a gun]."

Bee rode back to his soldiers. He was impressed by Jackson's determination. He spoke to his troops while pointing at Jackson, "Look, men! There is Jackson standing like a stone wall! Let us determine to die here, and we will conquer! Follow me!" Bee had given Thomas Jackson a nickname. From that point on, Jackson would always be known as "Stonewall" Jackson.

Part of the battlefield where the Union and Confederate armies fought at the First Battle of Bull Run

THOMAS J. JACKSON

Thomas Jonathan "Stonewall" Jackson was born in Virginia in 1824. His parents died when he was a boy. Relatives raised him. He started out at the U.S. Military Academy at West Point in 1842 as an awkward young man with a poor education. He had to struggle to keep his grades up. By the time he graduated in 1846, he had improved tremendously.

Jackson served in the Mexican War from 1846 to 1848 and fought bravely. While in Mexico, he became very devoted to the Christian faith. For the rest of his life, he never again smoked, drank, or played cards. He left the army in 1851 to become a teacher at the Virginia Military Institute (VMI). His cadets, or military students, thought he was boring and called him names behind his back. He took his cadets to Richmond in April 1861 so they could help train the new Virginia soldiers to fight for the Confederacy. Jackson left VMI during the Civil War to serve in the Confederate army. He was a much better officer than he was a teacher, and his soldiers admired him.

Jackson's first wife, Eleanor Junkin, died only fourteen months after their marriage. A few years later, Jackson married Mary Anna Morrison, a minister's daughter. They had two children, but only one survived. The other died of a fever in infancy.

General Thomas Jonathan Jackson, with hand on hip, *at the First Battle of Bull Run*

Soldiers' graves near Manassas, below. Although new to war, most of the soldiers mastered their fears and fought with great determination. A Georgia soldier wrote after the First Battle of Bull Run, "I felt that I was in the presence of death. My first thought was, 'This is unfair; somebody is to blame for getting us all killed. I didn't come out here to fight this way; I wish the earth would crack open and let me drop in.'"

A Union war reporter described the action at the First Battle of Bull Run, inset: "Men fall. . . . They are bleeding, torn, and mangled. . . . The trees are splintered, crushed, and broken, as if [hit] by thunderbolts. Twigs and leaves fall to the ground. There is smoke, dust, wild talking, shouting, hissings, howlings, explosions. It is a new, strange, unanticipated experience to the soldiers of both armies, far different from what they thought it would be."

Bee then bravely led his men forward, with their bayonets fixed to their muskets. The fighting went back and forth. In the end, the Confederates kept control of Henry House Hill.

More Confederate soldiers and cavalry (soldiers on horses) arrived. Union soldiers were getting tired. The Confederates were able to take control of the battlefield. So ended the Civil War's first major battle. The Union army retreated, or marched away, from the battle. Many were so scared that they ran away. The Union army retreated all the way back to Washington, D.C. The Confederate army slowly followed. In the First Battle of Bull Run, there were 2,896 Union casualties (soldiers who are killed, wounded, captured, or missing in battle). The Confederate army lost 1,982 men.

Before the First Battle of Bull Run, most people thought the war would end quickly. They thought soldiers would fight one battle and then come home. But this battle showed that the Civil War would be a long and bloody fight.

CHAPTER TWO

The *Monitor* and the *Virginia*

>—I—◆—O—◆—I—<

The First Battle of Bull Run showed Lincoln that he faced a hard fight against the South. Lincoln called Major General George B. McClellan to Washington, D.C., to take charge of all the Northern armies. McClellan became the North's general in chief—the general in charge of all other generals. McClellan was a brilliant organizer. He also took very good care

of his men. This made him popular. Whenever McClellan walked past his soldiers, they cheered loudly for him. McClellan named his army after a river near Washington, D.C. He called it the Army of the Potomac. McClellan spent months drilling, or training, the Army of the Potomac. He gathered weapons, horses, and supplies. By March of 1862, his army was ready to fight the Confederates.

McClellan planned to move his army by boat from Washington, D.C., to Fort Monroe. This fort was on the southeastern tip of a Virginia

peninsula (land with water on three sides). The James River ran along one side of the peninsula, and the York River along the other side. From Fort Monroe, McClellan's army would try to march into Virginia and capture Richmond. Ships in the Union navy would bring supplies to the army by sailing up the James and the York Rivers.

But there were two problems with McClellan's strategy. The peninsula was narrow, so a Confederate army could easily block, or stop, the Union army. To avoid this problem, McClellan and his soldiers would have to hurry. The second problem was a Confederate warship called the *Virginia*. The Confederates did not have a navy

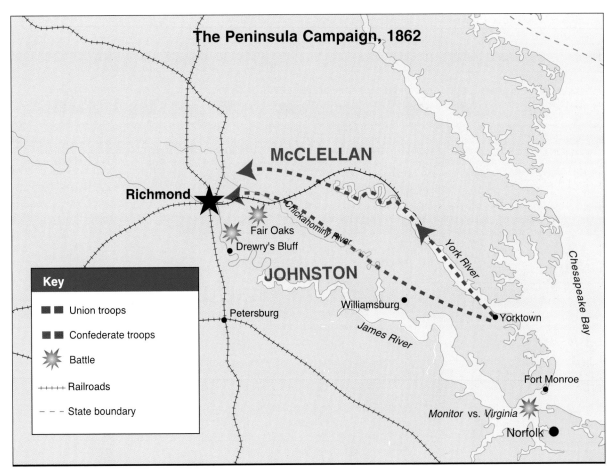

The Peninsula Campaign, 1862

McCLELLAN

Richmond

Fair Oaks
Drewry's Bluff

Chickahominy River

York River

Chesapeake Bay

JOHNSTON

Williamsburg

Petersburg

Yorktown

James River

Fort Monroe

Monitor vs. *Virginia*

Norfolk

Key

■ ■ Union troops

■ ■ Confederate troops

✴ Battle

+++++ Railroads

– – – State boundary

George B. McClellan

George Brinton McClellan was born in Pennsylvania in 1826, the son of a surgeon. He graduated near the top of his class at the U.S. Military Academy at West Point in 1846. A few months later, he joined the U.S. Army to fight in Mexico. During the Mexican War, he won three awards for his courage in battle. McClellan was a captain when he left the army in 1857. He got an important job at a railroad company in Illinois. There he met Abraham Lincoln, who worked as a lawyer for the same railroad.

At the beginning of the Civil War, McClellan was president of a railroad company in Ohio. Because of his brilliant early career in the army, the governor of Ohio put him in charge of the Ohio state militia (civilians who become soldiers during a war). In 1861 Lincoln put McClellan in charge of all the Union armies.

McClellan married Ellen Marcy, and they had two children. During his service in the Civil War, he wrote to her often and told her what was on his mind.

when the Civil War began. But they had captured the U.S. Navy's base in Norfolk, Virginia. There they had found an old, partly burned ship named the *Merrimack*. The *Merrimack* was built out of wood. It needed to be fixed. Confederate shipbuilders used their imagination. They fixed the *Merrimack* with iron instead of wood. Shipbuilders put iron armor (thick sheets of metal) on the sides and top of the *Merrimack*. They called this kind of ship an ironclad.

When the shipbuilders were done, they had created a boat that looked like a floating barn roof. The Confederates renamed their new ship the *Virginia*. The *Virginia* carried ten

The Confederates used the hull of the Merrimack *to build the ironclad* Virginia, *above.*

Ships moved up the James River and the York River, left, *bringing supplies to the Union army.*

29

The first commander of the Virginia, right, *was Franklin Buchanan. Before the Civil War, Buchanan had served in the U.S. Navy for many years. He had been the first superintendent of the U.S. Naval Academy in Annapolis, Maryland. Even with these ties to the North, the sixty-one-year-old Marylander believed that the South's cause was more just. He was seriously wounded in the* Virginia's *first fight.*

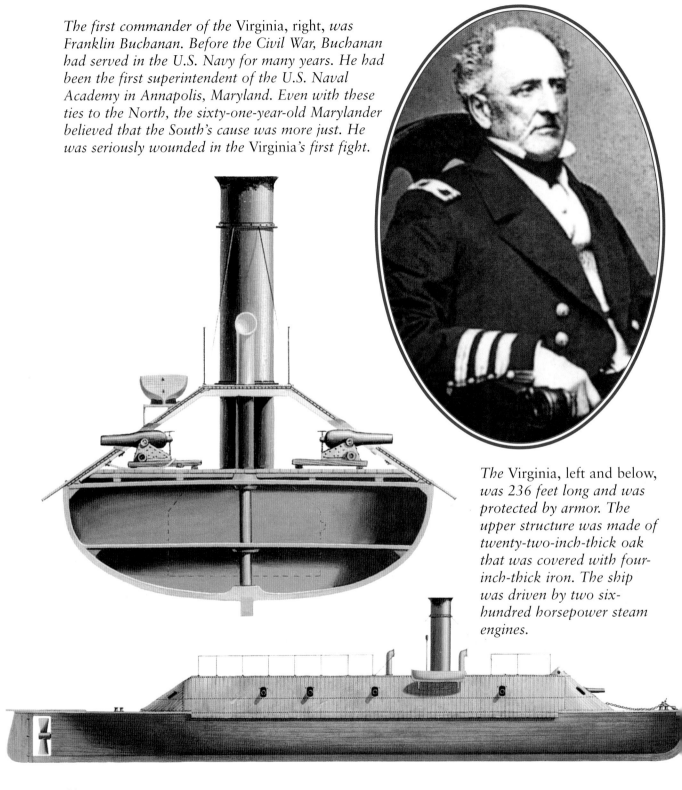

The Virginia, left and below, *was 236 feet long and was protected by armor. The upper structure was made of twenty-two-inch-thick oak that was covered with four-inch-thick iron. The ship was driven by two six-hundred horsepower steam engines.*

big guns. Four-inch-thick armor protected the 350 sailors inside. The boat had an iron prow, or rod, that could ram into an enemy ship and make a large hole. The hole let in water, and the enemy ship would sink.

But the _Virginia_ had three weaknesses. It moved slowly. It took thirty minutes to turn around. And it would get stuck in the bottom of the river unless the water was more than twenty-two feet deep.

Northern leaders planned to build an ironclad, too. An inventor named John Ericsson took the job. He had to work very quickly. In just 101 days, Ericsson and his team of shipbuilders finished the _Monitor._

The _Monitor_ had a nine-foot-tall iron turret, or tower, that held two guns. The turret was turned

Inside the gun turret (tower) of the Monitor

When the Virginia *first appeared, it seemed like a terrible monster. The* Monitor (right) *kept the monster from harming more Union ships.*

by a steam engine. Sailors could aim the two guns by turning the turret. The turret gave the *Monitor* an advantage over the *Virginia*. The *Virginia* did not have a turret. To aim its guns, the whole ship had to turn.

On March 8, 1862, the *Virginia* moved up the James River. It attacked two wooden Union ships: the *Congress* and the *Cumberland*. William Rebland, a twenty-year-old Union sailor from Michigan, was on the *Cumberland*. He described the *Virginia*: "As she came steaming up the river she was a grim-looking monster."

The pilot of the Cumberland *described the approach of the* Virginia, *inset:* "As she came ploughing through the water... she looked like a huge half-submerged crocodile."

The *Cumberland* and the *Congress* fired their cannons at the *Virginia*. But the shots bounced off the *Virginia*'s armor. The *Virginia* rammed and sank the *Cumberland*. The *Virginia*'s cannon fire forced the *Congress* to surrender, or give up.

The battle proved that wooden ships could not fight ironclads. Union officers worried that the *Virginia* would destroy the rest of the Union ships. Lincoln worried that the mighty *Virginia* might attack Washington, D.C., or New York City. Indeed, the *Virginia*'s new commander, Lieutenant Catesby Jones, planned to attack again. But the *Monitor* arrived to save the Union navy.

On March 9, 1862, the *Monitor* and the *Virginia* met. This was the first battle between ironclads. It lasted for two hours, but neither ship could sink the other. The shots from each ship just bounced off the other's iron sides. The battle ended without a winner.

The battle between the USS Monitor *and the CSS* Virginia *was the first fight between ironclads.*

CHAPTER THREE

To the Gates of Richmond

General Joseph E. Johnston was a very skilled general for the Confederacy. He commanded the Confederate army defending Richmond, Virginia.

On March 17, 1862, McClellan sent his army to Fort Monroe. He knew that the *Monitor* could protect his soldiers against the *Virginia.*

About three weeks later, on April 4, the Army of the Potomac started marching up the Virginia peninsula. The next day, 17,000 Confederate soldiers, led by General Joseph E. Johnston, blocked the Union army. The Confederates formed a line that was eight miles long. It ran from the York River to the James River. The Union army could not outflank the Confederates. But McClellan had 40,000 more soldiers than Johnston. If McClellan ordered an attack, his army could crash through the Confederate line.

Instead McClellan waited. He was a very cautious, careful commander who did not want his soldiers to die uselessly. McClellan spent the next few days watching the Confederate army and deciding what to do next.

Meanwhile, Jefferson Davis and other leaders in Richmond quickly sent thousands of men to help Johnston's Confederate line. The number of

Confederate soldiers grew from 17,000 to 60,000. The Confederates prepared for battle. They dug trenches, or ditches, to lie in and protect themselves. They placed long, sharp, wooden poles in the ground to stop enemy soldiers from getting near them. Their line was near Yorktown, Virginia. It became known as the Yorktown Line.

McClellan got ready for his attack. His men also dug trenches. Thousands of Union soldiers came to reinforce, or help, McClellan's army. They brought huge weapons, called siege guns, to blast a hole in the Confederate line.

Finally, by the beginning of May, McClellan's Army of the Potomac was ready. His 112,000

Union soldiers used huge mortars (siege guns) to fire at the Confederate army near Yorktown, Virginia.

Artillery and ammunition wait at the Yorktown, Virginia, wharf, opposite. These supplies eventually were shipped upriver to General McClellan's Union army at a base on territory that he controlled. The Union armies were much better supplied than the Confederate armies.

Union ships on the James River bombard the fort on Drewry's Bluff, Richmond, Virginia.

soldiers prepared to attack. Johnston did not think his army could win against such a huge force. On May 3, he ordered the Confederate army to leave the battlefield. The Confederate army retreated toward Richmond.

Johnston also ordered the *Virginia* to sail to Richmond. The *Virginia* tried, but it got stuck in the James River. The water was not deep enough. The Confederates could not leave their ironclad behind because the Union army might capture it. They had to blow up the *Virginia*.

Because the *Virginia* was gone, ships in the Union navy could sail up the James River toward Richmond. Seven miles from Richmond, on May 15, the Union navy attacked the Confederate fort on Drewry's Bluff.

But this time, the Confederates won. The fort on Drewry's Bluff was high above the water. The *Monitor* could not raise its guns high enough to fire at the fort. The Confederates fired artillery from the fort. The fire drove off the Union ships. The Union navy retreated and never attacked Drewry's Bluff again.

Meanwhile, McClellan's army kept marching up the peninsula toward Richmond. He met Johnston's Confederate army about ten miles outside of the city. The Army of the Potomac was much larger than the Confederate army. But instead of attacking, McClellan stopped. He planned his attack and waited for more Union soldiers to arrive.

Stonewall Jackson's Campaign
McClellan planned for a second Union army, led by General Irvin McDowell, to join the Army of the Potomac. If McDowell's men joined McClellan's men, the Union army would be big enough to capture Richmond. The Confederates would not be able to stop it.

Confederate leaders knew they were in trouble. They had to keep McDowell's army from joining McClellan's army. They saw only one hope: General Thomas "Stonewall" Jackson.

Jackson led a small group of soldiers in Virginia's Shenandoah Valley. The valley was important to the Confederates. It was a rich farming area. Farmers grew crops, such as wheat and corn, and raised animals, such as cows and pigs, which fed Confederate soldiers. But more important, the valley was a route, or way, for a Confederate army to threaten Washington, D.C. Jackson's mission was to

The ironclad USS Galena, opposite, *was one of the ships that fought at Drewry's Bluff, Virginia. The Marine corporal firing his musket won the Congressional Medal of Honor for his courage.*

A defeated Union army escapes from Stonewall Jackson. A Union officer complained about the Union generals who fought against Jackson: "I am heart-sick at the want [lack] of common sense."

make this threat and to keep McDowell and his army too busy to join McClellan.

Jackson had fought Union soldiers before. On March 23, 1862, he had attacked Union soldiers at Kernstown, Virginia, and lost. But his attack scared political leaders back in Washington, D.C. Lincoln worried that Jackson's army might invade the North and capture Washington, D.C.

During May and early June, Jackson moved his soldiers all around the Shenandoah Valley. His soldiers became known as "foot cavalry" because they marched as fast as if they were on horses. Jackson's men won many small battles against McDowell's army and stopped McDowell from reaching McClellan. Jackson's Shenandoah campaign, or series of battles, is remembered as one of the most brilliant in military history.

Meanwhile, near Richmond, McClellan was getting ready to attack. Union ships brought supplies and equipment, including heavy cannons, to the port of White House. This river town was about twelve miles away from McClellan's army. Trains brought the supplies to McClellan. To protect the trains, McClellan positioned, or placed, soldiers along the railroad. This spread out the Army of the Potomac and left it divided by the Chickahominy River.

Johnston saw an opportunity. Only part of McClellan's army was on the south side of the Chickahominy River. Johnston thought his men could defeat that group of Union soldiers. He attacked on May 31, 1862, at Fair Oaks, Virginia.

But Johnston's Confederate army had the same sort of problems that both Northern and

A Union observation balloon, called the Intrepid, *being filled with hot air. The Union army used the balloon to go up and see how the Confederate army was positioned for the Battle of Fair Oaks in Virginia.*

Southern armies had had at Bull Run. Generals did not know how to command large forces. They did not know how to work together. During the battle, soldiers did not know where to go. The Confederates lost the battle at Fair Oaks. Worse, Johnston was hurt badly.

Davis and other leaders of the Confederacy were very worried. The Union army was just outside their capital city. The Confederate army had been defeated. Johnston was too hurt to fight anymore. Davis made a decision that changed the course of the war. On June 1, 1862, he put General Robert E. Lee in charge of the Confederate army.

The Seven Days' Battles
Lee thought of a new, daring plan. He ordered Stonewall Jackson's army to move toward

Wounded Union soldiers being moved by train after the Battle of Fair Oaks

ROBERT E. LEE

Robert Edward Lee was born in Virginia in 1807. His father, "Light Horse Harry" Lee, had fought during the American Revolution (1775–1783). But by the time Lee was six years old, his father had lost all of his wealth and had left his family. At the age of twelve, Lee had to take care of the house and his mother, who was sick. Lee grew up to be a man of dignity, strength of character, and iron self-control.

In 1825 Lee went to the U.S. Military Academy at West Point and graduated second in his class. After his graduation in 1829, he chose the army as his career, or job. Lee received three awards for his bravery in the Mexican War and was well liked by his fellow soldiers. After the Mexican War, Lee was in charge of West Point for several years.

Lee married Mary Anna Randolph Custis, and they had seven children. But Lee rarely saw his wife and children because he was away at battle for years at a time.

Lee did not want Virginia to secede from, or leave, the United States. He said he would free all his slaves if it would save the nation from a war. But still, Virginia became part of the Confederacy. President Lincoln thought so well of Lee that he asked him to command the Union army. Instead, Lee joined the Confederate army. He was a Virginian and felt he could not go against his home state.

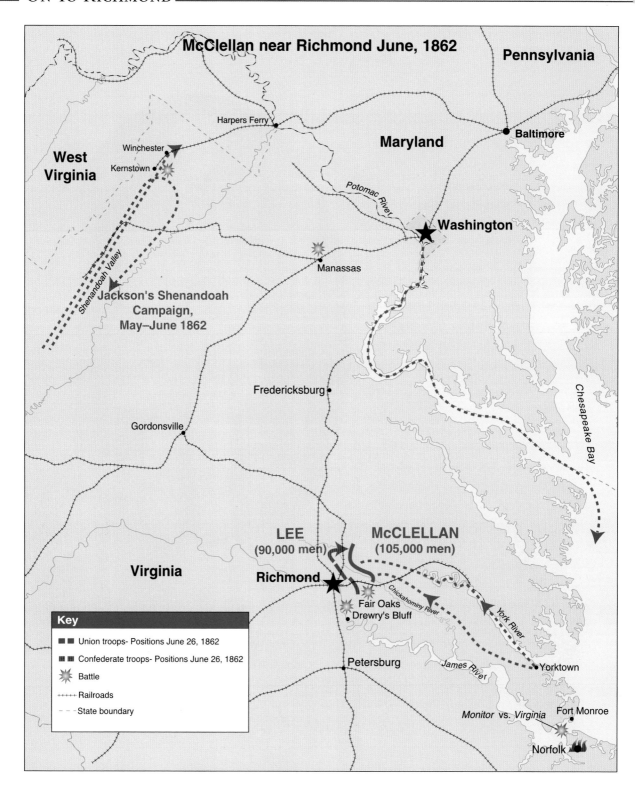

McClellan near Richmond June, 1862

Pennsylvania

Maryland

West Virginia

Harpers Ferry

Winchester

Kernstown

Baltimore

Potomac River

Washington

Manassas

Shenandoah Valley

Jackson's Shenandoah Campaign, May–June 1862

Chesapeake Bay

Fredericksburg

Gordonsville

Virginia

LEE (90,000 men)

McCLELLAN (105,000 men)

Richmond

Fair Oaks
Drewry's Bluff

Chickahominy River

York River

Key

■ ■ Union troops- Positions June 26, 1862

■ ■ Confederate troops- Positions June 26, 1862

✹ Battle

+++++ Railroads

- - - State boundary

Petersburg

James River

Yorktown

Monitor vs. Virginia

Fort Monroe

Norfolk

June 1862, opposite. General Jackson returned from the Shenandoah Valley to help General Lee defend Richmond.

General McClellan was a very cautious general. The Confederates fooled him by making logs look like cannons, below. Soldiers called these "cannons" Quaker guns because Quakers were peaceful people who didn't believe in fighting.

Richmond. Lee's army would attack McClellan's army from the front. Jackson's army would attack from the flank.

On June 25, 1862, the Seven Days' Battles began. Both armies still had many men who had never been in a battle. Both still had inexperienced officers. But the soldiers, whether fighting for the North or the South, proved themselves to be fierce warriors. The Seven Days' Battles were the biggest and bloodiest battles so far.

McClellan's army was still divided by the Chickahominy River. Lee ordered his army to attack Union soldiers who were north of the river. This was risky because Lee left only a few Confederate soldiers south of the Chickahominy River. McClellan's army could march quickly

along the south side and capture Richmond. But Lee understood McClellan. He knew McClellan was cautious and would wait to march toward Richmond.

Lee's attacks on June 26 and June 27 frightened McClellan. He ordered a retreat. But this was dangerous for the Union army. The land had many swamps, streams, and narrow roads. The Union army had to move very slowly.

Lee knew that this gave him a great chance. He hoped to destroy the Union army while it slowly retreated. But his plan failed. Just like every other leader so far, he could not get his generals to work together. Lee hoped Stonewall Jackson's men would move quickly. Instead, for the only

Thousands of Civil War soldiers were still in their teens. Edwin Jemison of Louisiana, opposite, was killed at age eighteen at the Battle of Malvern Hill, one of the Seven Days' Battles.

A Union cavalry charge at the battle of Gaines's Mill, below. This was the first big battle of the Seven Days' Battles. Six of the seven officers in the regiment were shot in this charge.

time in his career, Jackson moved slowly. A series of violent battles took place from June 28 to July 1. But McClellan's soldiers were able to escape.

Losses on both sides were heavy. Total casualties numbered more than 20,000 on the Confederate side. Union casualties were 16,000.

After the Seven Days' Battles, McClellan's army rested by the James River. Union ships on the river protected them. Lee's army had not destroyed McClellan's army. But the Confederates had moved the Union army thirty-five miles away from Richmond. The capital city of the Confederacy was safe for now.

THE CASUALTIES OF THE SEVEN DAYS' BATTLES

The Seven Days' Battles caused many casualties for the North and the South, as shown by the numbers below. CSA stands for the Confederate States of America (the Confederacy). USA stands for the United States of America (the Union).

June 25 Battle of Oak Grove—CSA win
USA 626 / CSA 441

June 26 Battle of Mechanicsville—CSA win
USA 361 / CSA 1,484

June 27–28 Battle of Gaines's Mill—CSA win
USA 6,837 / CSA 8,751

June 27–28 Battle of Garnett's and Golding's Farms—CSA win
USA 368 / CSA 461

June 29 Battle of Savage's Station and Allen's Farm—CSA win
USA 1,590 / CSA 626

June 30 Battle of White Oak Swamp—CSA win
USA 2,853 / CSA 3,615

July 1 Battle of Malvern Hill—USA win
USA 3,214 / CSA 5,355

Lessons of Battle

Lee and his generals had made mistakes during the Seven Days' Battles. But they had kept the Union army out of Richmond. Many of Lee's generals held important positions for the rest of the war. After the Seven Days' Battles, Lee knew that his best generals were Stonewall Jackson, James Longstreet, and J. E. B. "Jeb" Stuart.

Lee did not want to repeat the mistakes of the Seven Days' Battles. So he reorganized the Confederate army in a simpler and better way. All the infantry (soldiers who fought on foot) and most of the artillery (soldiers who handled the big guns) were in two big groups. Longstreet commanded one group and Jackson the other. Stuart commanded all of the cavalry. Lee also gave his army a name: the Army of Northern Virginia. The army would use this name for the rest of the war.

The Seven Days' Battles also changed the morale, or attitude, of soldiers from the North and the South. The Confederates had won the First Battle of Bull Run. They had defended Richmond and driven back the Yankees (Northeners) during the Seven Days' Battles. This gave the Confederates good morale. They trusted Lee and knew they could defeat Union soldiers.

General McClellan's army moving to a new base on the James River during the Seven Days' Battles

Soldiers on the march. Note the washed clothes hanging from the rifle. Men had to look after themselves and their supplies as well as they could.

Soldiers in the Union army had bad morale. They had lost at the First Battle of Bull Run and during the Seven Days' Battles. They still trusted McClellan, and they would still fight hard. But they were not sure that they could win the Civil War with McClellan in charge.

A Union officer explained how a good or bad general can affect morale: "The same men fight very differently, according to who commands them. If they have confidence in their commander, they will dash upon the enemy with an enthusiasm. . . for they know that. . . if they must die, their death will at least be useful to the cause. . . . But if they feel that they are being poorly led. . . their enthusiasm gives way to indecision."

The difference between the morale of the two armies made a big difference in future battles. The difference lasted until near the end of the war.

During the Seven Days' Battles, Lee showed that he was willing to take risks. He believed that to win the Civil War, the Confederates would have to be bold and daring. He knew soldiers would have to die to win battles. Lee kept this fighting attitude for the rest of the war.

Chapter Four

Lee Moves North

The Seven Days' Battles ended the immediate threat to Richmond. The action now shifted to the north.

The Army of the Potomac had low morale, but it was still powerful. A different leader might have attacked Richmond again. But McClellan did nothing. He was still cautious. Abraham Lincoln wondered if McClellan would ever fight.

Meanwhile, in Washington, D.C., Lincoln had learned some lessons from the Union defeats. Lincoln had tried to control events from Washington, D.C. He had failed. He had put McClellan in charge of all the Union armies. McClellan had failed. Lincoln realized that he needed someone new to command the Northern armies.

On July 11, 1862, Lincoln replaced McClellan with Major General Henry Halleck. Lincoln hoped Halleck would think up a good plan to defeat the South. After all, many people thought Halleck was a fine general. His nickname was "Old Brains."

Halleck took control of all the Union armies, but he still had generals working for him. McClellan still led one of the Union armies. And Lincoln put Major General John Pope in charge of a new army in the Shenandoah Valley and northern Virginia. Pope's mission was to protect Washington, D.C., to keep control of the Shenandoah Valley, and to help McClellan. Pope began by marching south from Washington, D.C., toward the important railroad junction of

Two days after the Union defeat at the Second Battle of Bull Run, the Confederates followed the Union army to Chantilly, Virginia. Union General Philip Kearny bravely charged the enemy, below, *and was killed. After the Battle of Chantilly, the Union army retreated to the defenses around Washington, D.C.*

Many Union soldiers did not like having General John Pope, above, *put in charge. A Union officer wrote:* "It can with truth be said of him that he had not a friend in his command from the smallest drummer boy to the highest general officer. All hated him."

Gordonsville, Virginia. That area was protected by Stonewall Jackson's Confederate army.

Pope's Union army had many more men than Jackson's. Lee took a risk. He sent reinforcements, or more soldiers, to Jackson. These reinforcements helped Jackson attack Pope's army. Like all Civil War generals, Jackson was still learning. He fought the Battle of Cedar Mountain on August 9, 1862, and made many mistakes. But Pope also made mistakes. The blundering battle decided nothing.

Meanwhile, Halleck asked McClellan to leave Virginia and return to the North. This decision gave Lee an opportunity. Since McClellan was leaving the Richmond area, Lee could send the rest of his soldiers to help Jackson fight Pope.

The result of this plan was the Second Battle of Bull Run. It took place in August 1862, where the North and South had fought in July 1861. Lee commanded the Confederates brilliantly. His top officers—Jackson, Longstreet, and Stuart—did very well.

Pope led the Union forces poorly. His army failed because he had not positioned soldiers well on the battlefield. His army suffered a major defeat and retreated back toward Washington, D.C.

For Lincoln, this was the worst yet. His hand-picked generals, Pope and Halleck, had been defeated. Now the Confederates might invade the North. The Union army had even lower morale. It was an emergency for the North. The North could lose the entire war in the next few weeks.

General Henry Halleck

CHAPTER FIVE

A Decisive Battle

Lincoln knew only one general still had the trust of the Army of the Potomac. Reluctantly, he put McClellan back in charge.

Lincoln knew that the Union soldiers trusted McClellan more than any other Northern general. Lincoln told an aide, "We must use what tools we have. There is no man in the Army who can [protect Washington, D.C.] and lick these troops of ours into shape half as well as he [McClellan]. . . . If he can't fight himself, he excels in making others ready to fight."

McClellan had been jealous of Pope and Halleck. He was happy to be back in charge. He proudly wrote to his wife, "Again I have been called upon to save the country."

Early in September, Lee and the Confederates moved across the Potomac River and into western Maryland. The Confederates were getting close to Washington, D.C. Lincoln sent McClellan and the Army of the Potomac to stop Lee's invasion of the North.

The Confederate move was another bold plan by Lee. The Army of Northern Virginia was worn out and ragged. They had fought many battles in the past ten weeks. The safe move would have been to go back to Richmond and rest. But Lee sensed that the North's morale was shaken. If he marched his army into the North, several good things might happen.

First, Lee's army could isolate, or separate, Washington, D.C., from the rest of the country. To do this, Lee's soldiers would block the Baltimore and Ohio Railroad. Then they would march to

Harrisburg, Pennsylvania, and burn the important railroad bridge across the Susquehanna River. Without railroads, Union soldiers could not leave Virginia and return North. They would not be able to defend Washington, D.C., from a Confederate invasion.

Second, Lee could help restart the cotton trade. Ever since the Civil War started, the North had stopped most Southern cotton from reaching Europe. European countries, such as France and England, were pro-South because they wanted the cotton trade to start again. If the Army of Northern Virginia won a battle in the North, France and England might send soldiers to help the Confederacy.

Third, and most important, Lee had a chance to win the Civil War. If his army successfully invaded the North, Lincoln and the Union might surrender.

For all these reasons, Davis and Lee agreed that an invasion of the North was worth the risk. To win, Lee decided, he had to march fast and far. But his soldiers were tired from marching and fighting. They didn't have much food left. A Maryland woman saw the Confederates march through her town: "Starvation...looked from their...eyes." All day they marched by, stopping only to beg for food. The amazed woman added, "That they could march or fight at all seemed incredible."

The news that General McClellan, on horse, was back in charge gave fresh hope to the tired, defeated Union soldiers. A captain remembered that the men "jumped to their feet, and sent up such a hurrah as the Army of the Potomac had never heard before." Another officer wrote that "McClellan possessed the confidence of his men and excited their enthusiasm in a higher degree than any commander the Army of the Potomac ever had."

Many men deserted, or left, the army to rest and look for food. Other Confederates refused to cross the Potomac River into Maryland. They wanted to defend the South, not invade the North. The deaths in earlier battles, the deserters, and the men who refused to cross the river left the Army of Northern Virginia with only about 55,000 men.

Lee split up his army. One group of soldiers stayed near Frederick, Maryland. The larger group, commanded by Stonewall Jackson, marched to surround Union soldiers in Harpers Ferry. Lee hoped to capture Harpers Ferry before McClellan noticed.

Unfortunately for Lee, McClellan had a piece of luck. Some of his soldiers were camped where Confederates had been days before. McClellan's men found a copy of Lee's orders, or plans. These orders described exactly how Lee had divided his army. McClellan read the orders and happily said, "If I cannot whip 'Bobbie Lee,' I will be willing to go home."

McClellan ordered his army to attack Lee. Union soldiers surprised the Confederates near Antietam Creek. If McClellan hurried, he could defeat Lee. But again, McClellan took his time. This was a mistake. It gave Lee time to get ready.

The Battle of Antietam

McClellan finally attacked as the sun came up on September 17, 1862. He sent part of his army toward the left side of Lee's army. Another part of the Union army went toward the right side. Confederate soldiers had to defend the right and the left sides at the same time. This left the center of the army open to attack. McClellan's soldiers tried to destroy Lee's army by charging (marching quickly) toward the center.

Battle of Antietam, September 17, 1862, opposite. Union forces made three major attacks: through the Cornfield, against Bloody Lane, and over Burnside's Bridge. At the end of the day, the Union forces had failed to drive the Confederates from the field.

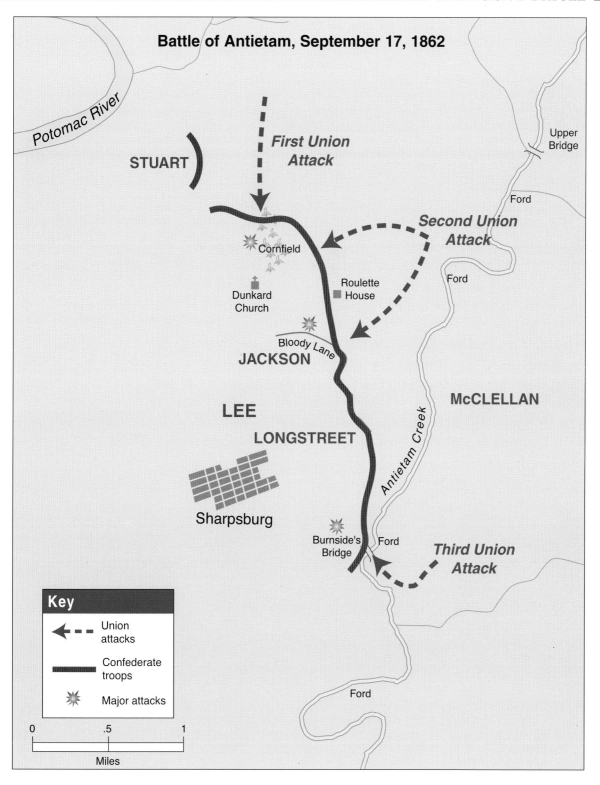

Battle of Antietam, September 17, 1862

Potomac River

STUART

First Union Attack

Cornfield

Second Union Attack

Dunkard Church

Roulette House

Bloody Lane

JACKSON

LEE

LONGSTREET

Sharpsburg

Antietam Creek

McCLELLAN

Upper Bridge

Ford

Ford

Burnside's Bridge

Ford

Third Union Attack

Ford

Key

Union attacks

Confederate troops

Major attacks

0   .5   1

Miles

Three times the Army of the Potomac almost destroyed Lee's army. But Lee's soldiers defended themselves bravely. The Union attacks did not work. McClellan's army fought hard, but it did not fight as a team. McClellan sent his soldiers into the fight only a few at a time.

By the end of the day, a huge number of Northern and Southern soldiers had been killed or wounded. Parts of the battlefield, such as Bloody Lane, were named because so many men died there. More American soldiers died or were wounded on this day than on any other day in any war ever fought by an American army. After the first day at Antietam, 26,134 men on both sides were either killed, wounded, captured, or missing.

Even though Lee and his army had lost a lot of soldiers, they stayed on the battlefield the next day just to show that they weren't afraid. McClellan believed his soldiers were too tired to attack again. But Lee knew that he had too few men to stay and fight another day. On the night of September 18, Lee and his army retreated back to Virginia.

After the Battle of Antietam, McClellan's army followed Lee's army. The end of the Civil War seemed far away. A Confederate officer sadly wrote to his wife: "Our victories. . . seem to settle nothing; to bring us no nearer the end of the war. It is only so many killed and wounded, leaving the work of blood to go on."

The Emancipation Proclamation

The Battle of Antietam was one of the most important battles of the war. It was the first time that the Army of the Potomac had forced Lee to retreat. This victory gave President Lincoln the chance to do something that completely changed the war.

President Lincoln, holding pen, *reads the Emancipation Proclamation to members of his cabinet (close advisers),* below.

A Union soldier reads the Emancipation Proclamation to a slave family, right. A Union officer remembered how the Emancipation Proclamation changed the war. "It was no longer a question of the Union. ... We were no longer merely the soldiers of a political controversy. ... We were now the missionaries of a great work...the armed liberators of millions [of slaves]."

On September 22, 1862, Lincoln issued a decree (order) called the Emancipation Proclamation. It would take effect on January 1, 1863. The proclamation freed all slaves in the Confederate states. Lincoln did this because Southern slaves were helping the Confederacy. Southern white men were able to leave their farms and factories to fight, because slaves did the work while they were away. Lincoln hoped that the freed slaves would leave and that the South's economy would collapse.

The Emancipation Proclamation changed the war from an effort to restore the United States to an effort to free the slaves. Abolitionists (those who are against slavery) were happy about this change. But many civilians and soldiers, in the North and the South, were not. They thought black people should remain slaves.

Lincoln Chooses Another General

McClellan was proud of what he had done at Antietam. His army had kept Confederates out of the North. He wrote to his wife "that I have done all that can be asked in twice saving the country."

But Lincoln wanted McClellan to do more. Defending the North was not enough. He told McClellan that he was too careful. He wanted McClellan to take risks like Lee was taking. Lincoln ordered McClellan to lead soldiers into the South and destroy Lee's army. But McClellan wouldn't listen. He found reasons to wait and would not do as Lincoln asked.

Lincoln was worried, and he was frustrated with McClellan. He became very thin and tired. One day, a friend of Lincoln's visited him at the army's camp. Lincoln asked his friend what he saw at the camp. The surprised friend said that he saw the Army of the Potomac. Lincoln replied, "So it is called, but that is a mistake; it is only McClellan's bodyguard [soldiers who protect one person instead of fighting battles]."

Lincoln decided he had had enough of McClellan. On November 7, 1862, he chose General Ambrose E. Burnside to replace McClellan as the leader of the Army of the Potomac.

President Lincoln (wearing top hat) *visits General McClellan and his staff after the Battle of Antietam.*

CHAPTER SIX

Defending Virginia Again

During the fall of 1862, Lee's soldiers rested. They became healthy and strong. They had enough food to eat. Deserters came back. New men joined the army. These were some of the best times for the Army of Northern Virginia. An officer remembered, "We began to feel that again we had an army." The 85,000 Confederate soldiers had high morale and began to believe that they "could not be whipped [beaten]."

But the Army of the Potomac had also grown bigger. By November 1862, Burnside commanded 120,000 men. He planned the Union army's next attack. His soldiers would march south and east to Fredericksburg, Virginia. They would cross the Rappahannock River and march right into Richmond. Burnside expected that Lee would rush south to defend Richmond. He hoped to defeat Lee's army while it was on the march.

The first part of Burnside's plan worked. The Union soldiers marched very quickly to Fredericksburg. Lee's army could not stop them. At the Rappahannock River, Burnside's men waited for pontoons, or floating bridges, to arrive. The soldiers planned to march across the pontoons to the other side of the river.

But the pontoons came too late. Lee had time to get his soldiers ready. The Confederates marched up a hill behind Fredericksburg. From the top of the hill, they could see all around them. No trees were in their way, so they could aim their guns right at the Union soldiers. The Confederate army was in an excellent spot.

Burnside should not have attacked the

Confederates. But he did not know what else to do. On December 13, the Army of the Potomac charged up the hill. A Confederate soldier on top of the hill described what he saw: "What a magnificent sight it is! We have never witnessed such a battle array [group] before. . . . It seemed like some blue [the color of Union soldiers' uniforms] serpent about to . . . crush us in its folds."

Wave after wave of brave Union soldiers ran up the hill. But the Confederates kept shooting at them with artillery and muskets. When an artillery shell hit the ground, it exploded and shot pieces of metal all around. A Union officer described his experience when a shell exploded in front of him. "One fragment [of metal] struck me just below the heart, making a bad wound. Another blew off my hat. Another small bit entered my mouth and

After the Battle of Fredericksburg, below, a Georgia soldier wrote, "We have given them [Union soldiers] the worst whipping that they ever got. It was a sight to see the battlefield. The dead [were] lying thick over about one hundred acres of ground."

broke out three of my best jawteeth, while the gravel, bits of frozen earth, and minute fragments of shell covered my face with bruises."

Union losses were huge. About 12,700 Union soldiers were casualties during the Battle of Fredericksburg. It was a terrible defeat for the North. Just like McClellan, Burnside had failed to destroy Lee's army. Union soldiers knew that they were as brave as the Confederates. But their generals had let them down. Lincoln knew this too. On January 25, 1863, Lincoln removed Burnside from command. Lincoln needed to find a new general to lead the Army of the Potomac.

General Lee, holding binoculars, and his staff at Fredericksburg. A Georgia soldier wrote home, "We never can be whipped while we have such a leader as General Lee."

It was very different on the Confederate side. The Confederate army had defeated the Union army at the First Battle of Bull Run, the Battle of Drewry's Bluff, the Seven Days' Battles, the Second Battle of Bull Run, and the Battle of Fredericksburg. The soldiers believed in Lee. They thought no one could beat them.

Both armies rested during the winter. But they would fight again in the spring of 1863.

A Civil War Army

How an Army Was Organized

A company was a small group of about 80 to 100 soldiers. Captains commanded the companies. Ten companies made up a regiment. The regiment was the basic unit of both infantry (soldiers on foot) and cavalry (soldiers on horseback).

The basic artillery unit was the battery. A battery had four to six guns. A full-strength battery could have as many as 156 soldiers. Captains also commanded batteries. Batteries were horse drawn, which means that horses pulled the guns and wagons to the battlefield. An average-sized battery included seventy horses and twenty-five mules. The artillery's job was to help the infantry by shooting at the enemy.

Four or more regiments made up a brigade. Brigadier generals commanded brigades. A group of three or more brigades made up a division. Major generals commanded divisions. Two or more divisions made an army corps. Senior generals commanded army corps. An army commander was in charge of the whole army.

Armies worked by following a chain of command. If an army commander wanted the army to march, he told the senior generals. They told the major generals, who told the brigadier generals, and so on. The order eventually reached the soldiers in the companies, but this took time.

Generals had helpers called staff officers. Staff officers had many important jobs. They had to make sure the soldiers had enough of everything they needed to fight, such as guns, ammunition, and uniforms. They also made sure soldiers, horses, and mules had enough food. Staff officers helped carry the generals' orders down the chain of command.

How an Army Marched

Soldiers might take a train or a boat to get to a battlefield. But most of the time, soldiers had to march along dirt roads. In dry weather, the marching soldiers kicked up a huge cloud of dust. In wet weather, the soldiers had to march slowly down the muddy roads.

Soldiers marched in ranks, or rows, along the road. The front rank was often only four men wide. Behind it came rank after rank, company after company, regiment after regiment. Mixed into the ranks were the artillery batteries. The supply wagons and the ambulances were in the back. A single division took up about two miles of road.

The generals and their staff officers had a hard time controlling the marching soldiers. When the roads were muddy or narrow, the soldiers would start and stop often. But when the roads were good, soldiers could march fast and far. Sometimes men marched thirty miles or more during a single day.

View of a typical Civil War battle scene from the rear. From front to back are wagon trains, reserve infantry, artillery, and the main battle line.

How an Army Fought

When an army got near the enemy, the soldiers deployed for battle. This meant they moved off the roads and formed into lines. Companies formed into lines with thirteen inches between each soldier. Each line was two ranks deep, which means one man stood behind another. When an officer gave an order, a company in line could move straight ahead or to either side.

A battlefield could be very confusing. When guns and cannons were shot, they let off a lot of smoke. Once the fighting started, the smoky air made if very difficult to see. Because there were so many soldiers, a general on a horse could see only a few of his men at a time. If he wanted to give an order, he had to shout or have a staff officer carry an order down the chain of command.

Most infantry soldiers carried guns called rifled muskets. The muskets were single-shot, which means that after each shot fired, the soldier had to reload.

Soldiers put each new bullet through the muzzle, or front, of the gun. The muskets were very long, so soldiers usually loaded while standing up. This was dangerous because their enemies could see them easily.

Artillery was a supporting, or helping, weapon. Artillery soldiers used cannons that could fire solid iron balls at the enemy. Cannons could fire shells, which were hollow, explosive missiles. Cannons could also fire canisters, which were containers holding many musket balls (bullets). The canisters exploded after the cannons fired. The musket balls spread out and hit many men at once.

Cavalry did not play a big role during a battle. Cavalry usually rode around the battlefield before the fighting started. They brought back information about where the enemy soldiers were. After the battle, they chased away the defeated enemy soldiers.

Time Line

April 14, 1861: The Confederates capture Fort Sumter in South Carolina.

April 20, 1861: Robert E. Lee joins the Confederate army, three days after his home state of Virginia secedes from the Union.

July 21, 1861: First Battle of Bull Run. The first real battle of the Civil War takes place on the banks of Bull Run, a creek near Manassas, Virginia.

March 9, 1862: The Confederate *Virginia* and the Union *Monitor* fight the first battle between ironclad ships. All shots bounce off the iron sides. Neither side wins.

March 23, 1862: Battle of Kernstown. General Thomas "Stonewall" Jackson attacks Union soldiers in Kernstown, Virginia. He loses the battle but badly frightens Union leaders.

May 15, 1862: Battle of Drewry's Bluff. The Union navy attacks a Confederate fort near Richmond, Virginia, but fails to capture it.

May 31–June 1, 1862: Battle of Fair Oaks. The Confederates attack Union soldiers in Fair Oaks, Virginia, but lose. Confederate General Joseph E. Johnston is badly wounded and has to be replaced.

June 1, 1862: Confederate president Jefferson Davis puts General Robert E. Lee in charge of the Confederate army.

June 25–July 1, 1862: Seven Days' Battles. Seven days of fighting in Virginia become known as the Seven Days' Battles. Confederate soldiers drive the Union army away from Richmond. Lee's troops grow more confident when they see that Lee is a good general.

August 29–30, 1862: Second Battle of Bull Run. Union forces are badly defeated.

September 17, 1862: Battle of Antietam. Lee and his army invade Maryland. The Union army stops them at Antietam Creek, near Sharpsburg, Maryland. More than 26,000 soldiers die or are wounded during the battle.

September 22, 1862: President Abraham Lincoln issues the Emancipation Proclamation. The proclamation says that all slaves in the Confederate states will be free on January 1, 1863.

November 7, 1862: President Lincoln removes General George B. McClellan from command of the Army of the Potomac and replaces him with General Ambrose E. Burnside.

December 13, 1862: Battle of Fredericksburg. General Burnside orders the Army of the Potomac to attack General Lee's army at Fredericksburg, Virginia. The Union suffers a terrible defeat.

January 25, 1863: President Lincoln removes General Burnside from command. Lincoln tries to find a new general to lead the Army of the Potomac.

Notes

For quoted material in text:

p. 10, Bell Irvin Wiley, *The Life of Johnny Reb: The Common Soldier of the Confederacy* (Baton Rouge, LA: Louisiana State University Press, 1978), 29.

p. 16, Bell Irvin Wiley, *The Life of Billy Yank: The Common Soldier of the Union* (Baton Rouge, LA: Louisiana State University Press, 1978), 70.

p. 17, William C. Davis, *Battle at Bull Run* (Garden City, NY: Doubleday and Co., 1977), 178–79.

p. 18, James I. Robertson, *Stonewall Jackson: The Man, the Soldier, the Legend* (New York: Macmillan Publishing, 1997), 264.

p. 19, Ibid.

p. 19, Ibid.

p. 32, *Voices of the Civil War: The Peninsula* (Alexandria, VA: Time-Life Books, 1997), 46.

p. 51, P. Regis De Trobriand, *Four Years with the Army of the Potomac* (Boston: Ticknor and Co., 1889), 546–47.

p. 54, Michael Burlingame and John R. Turner Ettlinger, *Inside Lincoln's White House: The Complete Civil War Diary of John Hay* (Carbondale, IL: Southern Illinois University Press, 1997), 38, 39.

p. 54, George B. McClellan to Ellen McClellan, 5 September 1862, in Stephen W. Sears, *The Civil War Papers of George B. McClellan: Selected Correspondence, 1860–1865* (New York: Ticknor and Fields, 1989), 435.

p. 55, *Battles and Leaders of the Civil War* (New York: Thomas Yoseloff, 1956), 2: 687–88.

p. 55, Ibid.

p. 56, John Gibbon, *Personal Recollections of the Civil War* (Dayton, OH: Morningside Bookshop, 1978), 73.

p. 58, Frank Paxton to Elizabeth Paxton, 12 October 1862, in John Gallatin Paxton, *The Civil War Letters of Frank "Bull" Paxton, C.S.A.* (Hillsboro, TX: Hill Jr. College Press, 1978), 58.

p. 60, George B. McClellan to Ellen McClellan, 20 September 1862, in Sears, *The Civil War Papers of George B. McClellan*, 476.

p. 60, John G. Nicolay and John Hay, *Abraham Lincoln: A History* (New York: Century Co., 1890), 6: 175.

p. 61, Gary W. Gallagher, *Fighting for the Confederacy: The Personal Recollections of General Porter Alexander* (Chapel Hill, NC: University of North Carolina Press, 1989), 155.

p. 61, Ibid.

p. 62, Richard Wheeler, *Lee's Terrible Swift Sword: From Antietam to Chancellorsville: An Eyewitness History* (New York: HarperCollins Publishers, 1992), 284.

p. 62, Ibid., 287.

For quoted material in captions:

p. 11, Wiley, *The Life of Johnny Reb: The Common Soldier of the Confederacy*, 29.

p. 13, *Battles and Leaders of the Civil War*, 1: 154–55.

p. 15, Bruce Catton, *The Coming Fury* (Garden City, NY: Doubleday and Co., 1961), 402.

p. 22, Davis, *Battle at Bull Run*, 177–78.

p. 23, Charles Carleton Coffin, *My Days and Nights on the Battlefield* (Boston: Estes and Lauriat, 1887), 46.

p. 25, Gibbon, *Personal Recollections of the Civil War*, 10.

p. 33, Richard Wheeler, *Sword over Richmond: An Eyewitness History of McClellan's Peninsula Campaign* (New York: Harper and Row, 1986), 78.

p. 42, Milo M. Quaife, ed., *From the Cannon's Mouth: The Civil War Letters of General Alpheus S. Williams* (Detroit, MI: Wayne State University Press, 1959), 97.

p. 53, Ibid., 111.

p. 55, *Battles and Leaders of the Civil War*, 2: 490.

p. 55, Gibbon, *Personal Recollections of the Civil War*, 94.

p. 59, Trobriand, *Four Years with the Army of the Potomac*, 391, 396.

p. 62, J. Roderick Heller III and Carolynn Ayres Heller, eds., *The Confederacy Is on Her Way Up the Spout: Letters to South Carolina, 1861–1864* (Athens, GA: University of Georgia Press, 1992), 82–83.

p. 63, Ibid., 91.

➤·❀·➤·❍·❮·❀·❮

Selected Bibliography

Battles and Leaders of the Civil War. Vols. 1 and 2. New York: Thomas Yoseloff, 1956.

Boatner, Mark Mayo, III. *The Civil War Dictionary*. New York: David McKay Co., 1959.

Catton, Bruce. *Mr. Lincoln's Army*. Garden City, NY: Doubleday and Co., 1951.

Davis, William C. *Battle at Bull Run*. Garden City, NY: Doubleday and Co., 1977.

Esposito, Vincent J., ed. *The West Point Atlas of American Wars*. Vol. 1. New York: Frederick A. Praeger Publishers, 1959.

Gibbon, John. *Personal Recollections of the Civil War*. Dayton, OH: Morningside Bookshop, 1978.

McPherson, James M. *Battle Cry of Freedom: The Civil War Era*. New York: Oxford University Press, 1988.

Quaife, Milo M., ed. *From the Cannon's Mouth: The Civil War Letters of General Alpheus S. Williams*. Detroit, MI: Wayne State University Press, 1959.

Sears, Stephen W. *The Civil War Papers of George B. McClellan: Selected Correspondence, 1860–1865*. New York: Ticknor and Fields, 1989.

Wheeler, Richard. *Lee's Terrible Swift Sword: From Antietam to Chancellorsville: An Eyewitness History*. New York: HarperCollins Publishers, 1992.

Wiley, Bell Irvin. *The Life of Billy Yank: The Common Soldier of the Union*. Baton Rouge, LA: Louisiana State University Press, 1978.

———. *The Life of Johnny Reb: The Common Soldier of the Confederacy*. Baton Rouge, LA: Louisiana State University Press, 1978.

Williams, T. Harry. *Lincoln and His Generals*. New York: Alfred A. Knopf, 1952.

For More Information

Books

Burchard, Peter. *Lincoln and Slavery*. New York: Atheneum, 1999.

Carter, Alden R. *Battle of the Ironclads: The* Monitor *and the* Merrimack. New York: Franklin Watts, 1993.

Clinton, Catherine. *Scholastic Encyclopedia of the Civil War*. New York: Scholastic, Inc., 1999.

Day, Nancy. *Your Travel Guide to Civil War America*. Minneapolis: Runestone Press, 2001.

Dolan, Edward F. *The American Civil War: A House Divided*. Brookfield, CT: Millbrook Press, 1997.

Freedman, Russell. *Lincoln: A Photobiography*. New York: Clarion Books, 1987.

Grabowski, Patricia. *Robert E. Lee*. Philadelphia: Chelsea House, 2000.

Hakim, Joy. *War, Terrible War*. New York: Oxford University Press, 1994.

Hughes, Chris. *Antietam*. Brookfield, CT: Millbrook Press, 1998.

January, Brendan. *The Emancipation Proclamation*. New York: Children's Press, 1997.

Marrin, Albert. *Unconditional Surrender: U.S. Grant and the Civil War*. New York: Atheneum, 1994.

Pflueger, Lynda. *Stonewall Jackson: Confederate General*. Springfield, NJ: Enslow, 1997.

Ransom, Candace. *Children of the Civil War*. Minneapolis: Carolrhoda Books, 1998.

Smith, Carter, ed. *The First Battles: A Sourcebook on the Civil War*. Brookfield, CT: Millbrook Press, 1993.

Video

The Civil War. Walpole, NH: Florentine Films, 1990. Videocassette series. This PBS series by Ken Burns and narrated by David McCullough includes personal accounts and archival photos, as well as commentary by many writers on the period.

Civil War Journal. New York: A & E Networks, 1993. Videocassette series. Includes diaries and reenactments.

Web Sites

<http://www.ajkids.com>
> Users can ask questions about U.S. history in plain language and get connected to several different sites with answers.

<http://www.enteract.com/~westwood>
> Antietam: A Photographic Tour

<http://www.nps.gov/mana/home.htm>
> The home page for the Manassas National Battlefield, which includes some activities for students.

Places to Visit

Antietam National Battlefield, Sharpsburg, Maryland. More than nine hundred acres of the actual ground where the fighting occurred, with markers explaining the action.

Fort Ward Museum, Alexandria, Virginia. One of several forts that defended the approaches to Washington, D.C. It has exhibits of Civil War weapons and uniforms.

Fredericksburg National Military Park, Fredericksburg, Virginia. More than eight thousand acres covering the sites of four different battles, with markers explaining the action.

Manassas National Battlefield, Manassas, Virginia. More than five thousand acres covering the sites of the First and Second Battles of Bull Run.

Museum of the Confederacy, Richmond, Virginia. A huge collection of flags, uniforms, weapons, equipment, and paintings of Confederates. It is next door to the house where Jefferson Davis lived while president of the Confederacy.

Index

A Union battery in 1861

About the Authors

James R. Arnold was born in Illinois, and his family moved to Switzerland when he was a teenager. His fascination with the history of war was born on the battlefields of Europe. He returned to the United States for his college education. For the past twenty-five years, he and his wife, Roberta Wiener, have lived and farmed in the Shenandoah Valley of Virginia and toured all the Civil War battlefields.

Mr. Arnold's great-great-grandfather was shot and killed in Fairfax, Virginia, because he voted against secession. Another ancestor served in an Ohio regiment during the Civil War. Mr. Arnold has written more than twenty books about American and European wars, and he has contributed to many others.

Roberta Wiener grew up in Pennsylvania and completed her education in Washington, D.C. After many years of touring battlefields and researching books with her husband, James R. Arnold, she has said, "The more I learn about war, the more fascinating it becomes." Ms. Wiener has coauthored nine books with Mr. Arnold and edited numerous educational books, including a children's encyclopedia. She has also worked as an archivist for the U.S. Army.

>—+◆>—◦—<◆+—<

Picture Acknowledgments

Antietam National Battlefield: 54-55. *Frank Leslie's Illustrated Newspaper*: 31, 65. Library of Congress: back cover, 6, 8, 11, 12-13, 14, 15, 27, 28-29, 30T, 32-33, 37, 38, 39, 42, 44, 47, 49, 50, 71-72. Maryland Historical Society: front cover. Military Archive & Research Services, England: 34-35, 62. National Archives: 9, 16, 20, 21, 22-23, 24-25, 36, 43, 45, 48, 51, 52-53, 53T, 53B, 60, 63. Naval Historical Center, Washington, DC: 33. U.S. Army Military Institute: 18-19. U.S. Marine Corps, Washington, D.C.: 41. U.S. Military Academy: 6-7, 59. U.S. Senate Collection: 58-59. Virginia Military Institute: 10. West Point Museum Collection, *"Corporal John Mackie, USMC,"* 1988, by Charles Waterhouse. Property of the History and Museums Division,

Maps by Jerry Malone and Tim Kissel.